MY BODY IS PRIVATE

Other Books by Linda Walvoord Girard
Who Is a Stranger and What Should I Do?
You Were Born on Your Very First Birthday

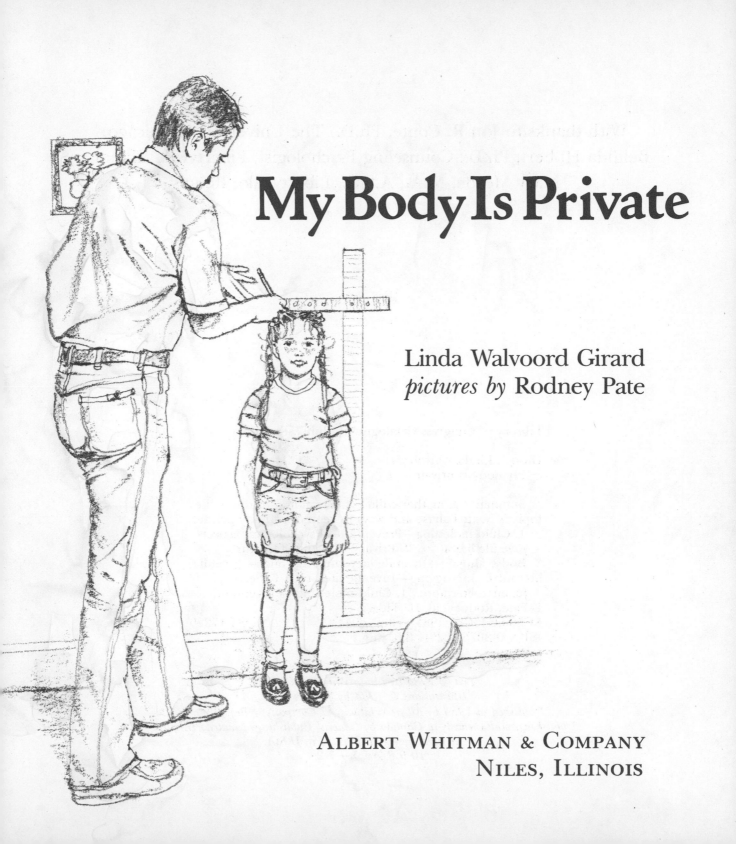

My Body Is Private

Linda Walvoord Girard
pictures by Rodney Pate

ALBERT WHITMAN & COMPANY
NILES, ILLINOIS

With thanks to Jon R. Conte, Ph.D., The University of Chicago; Belinda Hubert, Ph.D., Counseling Psychologist, Libertyville, Illinois; Mary Meade, M.A., A.S.C., Libertyville, Illinois.

Library of Congress Cataloging in Publication Data

Girard, Linda Walvoord.
   My body is private.

   Summary: A mother-child conversation introduces the topic of sexual abuse and ways to keep one's body private.
   1. Child molesting—Prevention—Psychological aspects —Juvenile literature. 2. Privacy—Juvenile literature. 3. Body, Human—Juvenile literature. 4. Touch—Juvenile literature. 5. Hugging—Juvenile literature. 6. Secrecy —Juvenile literature. [1. Child molesting—Prevention] I. Pate, Rodney, ill. II. Title.
RC560.C46G57 1984   362.7'044   84-17220
ISBN 0-8075-5320-4 (lib. bdg.)

For the Creekmurs, the Merkovskys,
Jamie Panko, and Jacqueline Thomas. R.P.

Some things in the world are private!

Whatever has my name—Julie—on it is mine.
That means don't touch and do not disturb,
unless I say you can.

"Nobody else uses my toothbrush,"
I told my brother Rob. "It's private."

"Yuk," he said. "Who'd want to?"

Today a letter came for me!
Nobody else opened it. I got to do that.
A person's mail is private.
It was an invitation to Susan's birthday party.
Not even my dad knew what it was, until I told him.

At our house, when any door is closed,
it means, "Private! Please knock!"
My brother Rob has his own room. It's private.
He can look in the mirror
and comb his hair all day, if he wants.

My parents close the door to their room sometimes.

If the door to my room is closed,
that means I want to be by myself.
I can read a book or watch my goldfish eat
or sit on the rug and do nothing.

My body is private, too.
My mom says that everything covered by my bathing suit—
my breasts, my vagina, and my bottom—is very private.
Nobody should touch me in those places
unless there's a very good reason.
A boy's penis and bottom are very private, too.

My baby brother's body is private,
but he still has to have his diapers changed and
he can't take baths by himself. Someone has to touch
the private parts of his body, to take care of him.

I'm not a baby anymore.
Most of the time I can take care of myself.
Sometimes the doctor has to touch
my bottom for a check-up.
But my mom asked him to tell me first
if he's going to do that.

My mom and dad say if anyone else starts
to touch me—anyplace—
and I don't like it,
I can say, "No!"

Most of the time I like to be touched.
Mom hugs me when I sit on her lap.
I cuddle my dog, Red. Red likes it, I can tell.

My baby brother likes to kiss me.

Dad and I like to dance.
He's teaching me the old-fashioned way.

I sit close to my babysitter for stories.
It makes the stories better, snuggling up.
And I like to hug my teacher.

But sometimes touching doesn't feel good.
Last night Rob tickled me more and more
until I could hardly get my breath.
At first it was fun.
But then my stomach started to hurt.
He had my arms pinned.
"Stop!" I said.
He kept right on. "Stop! Stop!" I yelled.

"Rob, stop it now," Dad said.
"Julie doesn't like it anymore."
"Aw, it's only a game," Rob said.

"In this family," Dad said, "with any kind of touching,
if somebody says stop, that means stop."

"Okay, kid, you're free." Rob went off to do his homework.
"Thanks, Dad," I said. He ruffled my hair.
I'm glad Dad made Rob stop.
I love my brother. But sometimes even your own family
and friends don't think how you might feel about touching.

Take Uncle Ted. He's my dad's brother.
He comes over to our house
and brings us peppermints, which I love.
But I don't want to get too close to Uncle Ted.

Uncle Ted used to sit me on his lap
and pat and rub my arms.
Pat, pat. Rub, rub. It didn't feel good.
And he smelled like tobacco.
After the last time Uncle Ted was here,
I asked my mom, "Do I have to let Uncle Ted
put me on his lap? I don't like it."

"Of course you don't have to," she said. "You can say no."

"But Uncle Ted will think I don't like him."

Mom frowned. "The important thing is your feelings.
Uncle Ted will understand.
I could tell him for you, but I think you can do it.
Just say, 'No, thanks, I don't want to.'"

The next time Uncle Ted came over,
he started to put me on his lap.
Out came his arm, curling toward me.

"No, thanks," I said. "I don't want to."
I stepped away. Uncle Ted stared at me.
My heart was pounding.

"Too big for me, huh?" he said.
He was smiling. "Okay, princess."

I couldn't believe it.
He didn't seem mad at all.
I didn't know I could make Uncle Ted stop.
But I could.

When he left, he patted my head
to show he was still my friend.

I talked to my mom about what happened.
"I'm proud of you, Julie, for sticking up
for your feelings," my mom said.
"If you don't feel good about the way someone
is touching you, you can tell that person to stop."

"Did Uncle Ted do anything wrong, Mom?"

"No," she said. "He just didn't know how you felt.
That's why you had to tell him.
But it would have been wrong if he kept on
touching you when you asked him to stop."

"And it's wrong if grownups or older kids try
to touch or rub the private parts of your body—
your breasts or your vagina or your bottom.
It's wrong if anyone says,
'Pull down your pants,'
or pulls down theirs,
or if someone wants to take a picture of you
without your clothes on."

"Ugh," I said. "Who'd ever try to do that?"

"It might be a stranger, or it might be
someone you know, like a babysitter, a teacher,
or a friend," Mom said, "or even someone
in our family. It probably won't ever happen.
You don't need to worry about it;
you just need to know what to do—
the way you know what to do if a fire starts."

"I'd get mad," I told Mom.
"I'd shout NO and run away."

"Good!" she said.
"And you must come and tell me what happened.
Sometimes it's hard to make a person stop acting that way.
He or she might pretend it's a game or
say you'll get in trouble if you tell.
The person might try to scare you.
But if someone touches the private parts of your body,
I want to know. No matter how scared you are,
no matter who it is—I don't care if it's Santa Claus—
you tell me.
And if I'm not around, tell Daddy or your teacher
or some other grownup you trust.
If one person doesn't believe you, tell someone else.
Never be afraid to tell.
No matter what happened, it's not your fault.
You won't get into trouble."

"Mom!" I said. "I'd never keep a secret like that."

"That's my smart girl," Mom said.
"If you keep it a secret, no one can help.
Now hurry and get ready for bed."

I put on my nightgown and brushed my teeth.
Then Dad rode me piggyback to my room.
He pretended I was too heavy for him.
"Oooof!" he said.
"I think you're bigger than you were last night.
Pretty soon you'll be all grown up."

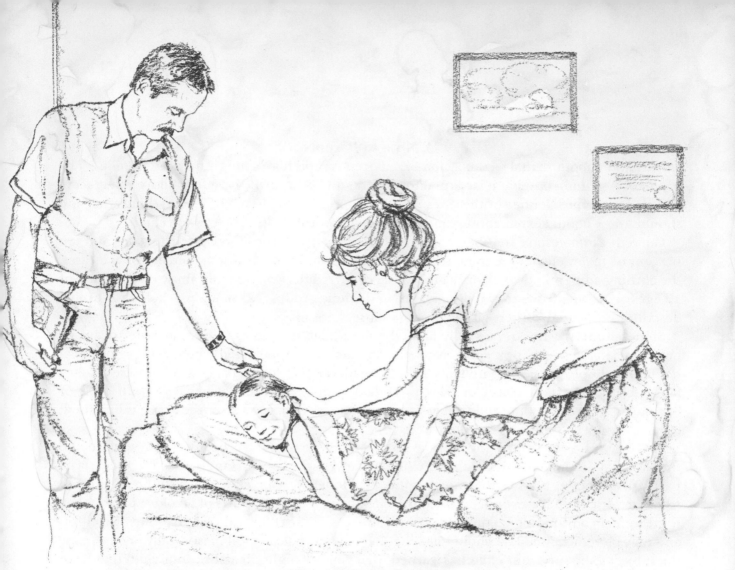

I *am* growing up.
I know what private means,
and I know what I'd do if someone tried
to touch the private parts of my body. I'd tell!

I gave my mom and dad a goodnight hug.
I'm glad most touching is good.
It's wonderful to throw your arms around people you love.

A Note to Parents

Information about sexual victimization of children is rapidly reaching American families. The problem is so immense that it is natural for parents and others who care for children to react in disbelief or panic. Neither of these responses is appropriate. There are several things that you should know about sexual abuse and several ways you can help protect your child.

Current estimates are that before age eighteen, twenty to forty percent of females and ten percent of males encounter some form of sexual abuse. In about ninety percent of the cases, the abusing adult is known by or related to the child. Adults who sexually abuse children are of all ages and come from all racial, religious, and ethnic groups. No single psychological profile describes the sexual abuser, although most abusers are male.

Some children who are sexually abused will exhibit symptoms. These include: dramatic behavior changes (a happy child may become quiet and appear sad); behavior problems at home or school; physical complaints such as headaches or stomachaches; nightmares; reluctance to go to certain places or be with certain people; and sexual behavior with dolls or playmates. However, some children will only show these behaviors after the abuse is disclosed; others will never show any symptoms.

Talking with your child is the best way to find out if he or she has been sexually abused and the best way to prevent sexual abuse. Using whatever words your family uses for the private parts of the body, ask whether anyone has ever touched your child's private body parts or whether your child has ever been asked to touch the private body parts of an older person. You need to feel comfortable talking about this subject or your child will pick up your discomfort and may be reluctant to talk about touching. Remember that you will periodically need to raise the subject to be sure your child has learned what you've taught. Reassure your child that he or she will not get into trouble for telling you about any kind of sexual abuse.

Above all, believe your child if he or she reports abuse. **If your** child tells you that someone has touched his or her body in ways that seem inappropria**te, you** should have your child seen by a mental health counselor who can help determine what happened, help you and your child recover, and help you decide if a report should be made to your state Child Protection Agency. Remember that most children who are abused can recover completely.

By talking to your child, you can help prevent sexual abuse! For more information, write: Sexual Abuse Prevention, National Committee for the Prevention of Child Abuse, Post Office Box 2866, Chicago, IL 60690.

Jon R. Conte, Ph.D., The University of Chicago